Wildwood Devotions

poems || asemics

Wildwood Devotions

poems || asemics

Karla Van Vliet

SHANTI ARTS PUBLISHING
BRUNSWICK, MAINE

Wildwood Devotions: poems || asemics

Published by Shanti Arts Publishing

Interior and cover design by Karla Van Vliet

Cover image: Karla Van Vliet,
Singing with the Nightingale

Shanti Arts LLC
193 Hillside Road
Brunswick, Maine 04011
shantiarts.com

Printed in the United States of America

ISBN: 978-1-962082-39-6 (softcover)

Thank you to the asemic/vispo community, especially to the many women, Kristine Snodgrass in particular, who are expanding the genre in so many ways, giving space for all to bring forth one's creative voice.

Other Books by Karla Van Vliet

She Speaks Tongues: poems || asemic writing

Fluency: A Collection of Asemic Writing

The River From My Mouth

From the Book of Remembrance

Chapbooks

Fragments: From the Lost Book of the Bird Spirit

Bone Scribed: poems || asemics

Colors of the Grittiest God,
a collaboration with Kristine Snodgrass

Contents

Acknowledgments

The following poems previously appeared in these publications:

Hidden Noise: "Bound (for)" (first published as "Under the Blue-Dark Sky"

deLuge Journal: "Dry Spell" and "All Night a Sky Full of Rain"

Crannog Magazine: "Song of the Birds"; "At the Sink" and "Second Thoughts"

Tishman Review: "Night Swan"

Heartwood: "Off Season, Hallowed"

Blue Herron Review: "Unstitched"

Green Mountains Review: "Yielding"

Orbis: "In the Rain Grayed Evening, A Snowy Egret"

Thank you to the many who support my creative explorations. To my family, my loved ones (you know who you are,) Sue Scavo, Kristine Snodgrass, Liz Powell, Adrie Kusserow, and the amazing asemic community.

I would especially like to thank Christine Cote of Shanti Arts who has, time and again, offered to bring my work into the world. You have been the most gracious conduit, thank you.

In the days I find it hard to bring forth, in words, what needs saying, I turn to asemics. For me asemics hold the space between the spoken and not spoken. The rising; like mist in the valley before it disperses into sky.

The asemic paintings within are part of my *Winter Dreamtime* series; caught in the time of hibernation, the mysterious interior.

asemic (visual poetry)

From the Minnesota Center for Book Arts: "Asemic writing is a wordless semantic form that often has the appearance of abstract calligraphy. It allows writers to present visual narratives that move beyond language and are open to interpretation, relying on the viewer for context and meaning."

Bound (for)

She stands in night's cold,
arms drawn close,
the full moon's light
littering the ground.
If only the deer
would come out
of the woods, surround
her, turn her gentle, turn
her tender, or the wolf
on the ridge meet her cry
with his own, and if not
the wolf the barred owl,
and if not that rare creature
the flaming holy that cowers
in the cradle of her chest.
Might that light dare
blaze, burn through
the tied knots drawn taut.

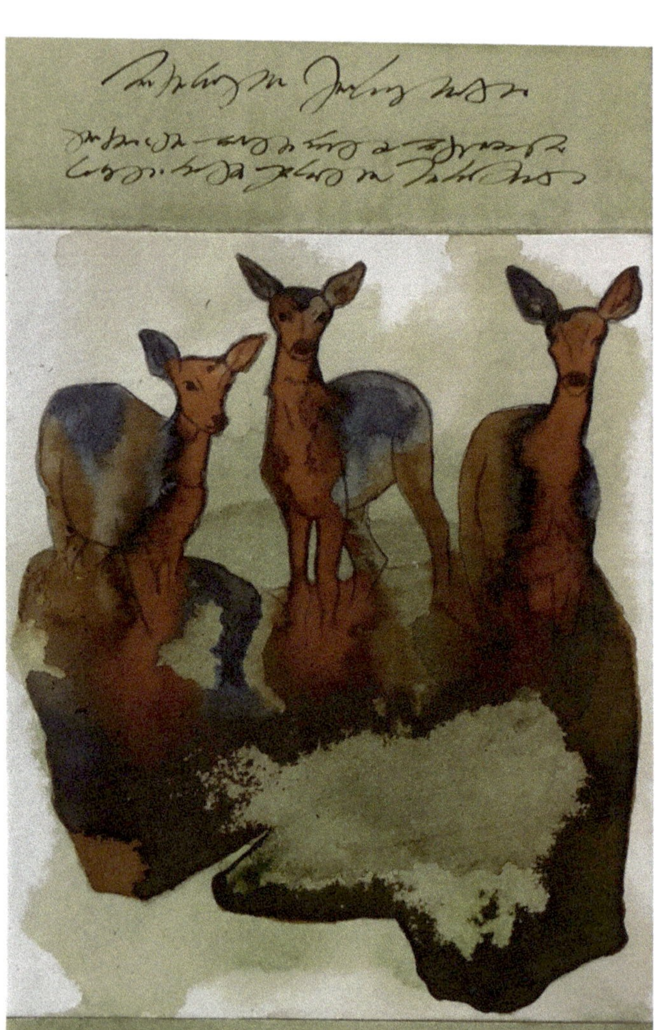

three visitors bringing gifts

Hallowed

The girl prays, her hands the form of a wolf
as if to reconstruct the shape of him,
her face in his pelt, his scent the wet earth
of den, of sanctum; prays holy, holy,
his body's wild offering, its mystery a fire set
in her belly, such raging flames, candescence,
curling licks consuming the dry tinder –
what grows, from ash, the heat cracked shell,
her voice rises both desolate and according;
cast alms in the mountain's bowl.

Remains

All day, mouthfuls of silence,
depths of water, of milky way.

All day, your memory's heft.
Figure like a fish in a pool, a

shadowed undercut. Bluets quicken
early sky, a glimpsed shimmering, a

hand graze, rushes in wind, a
thousand bodies, all day,
bowing.

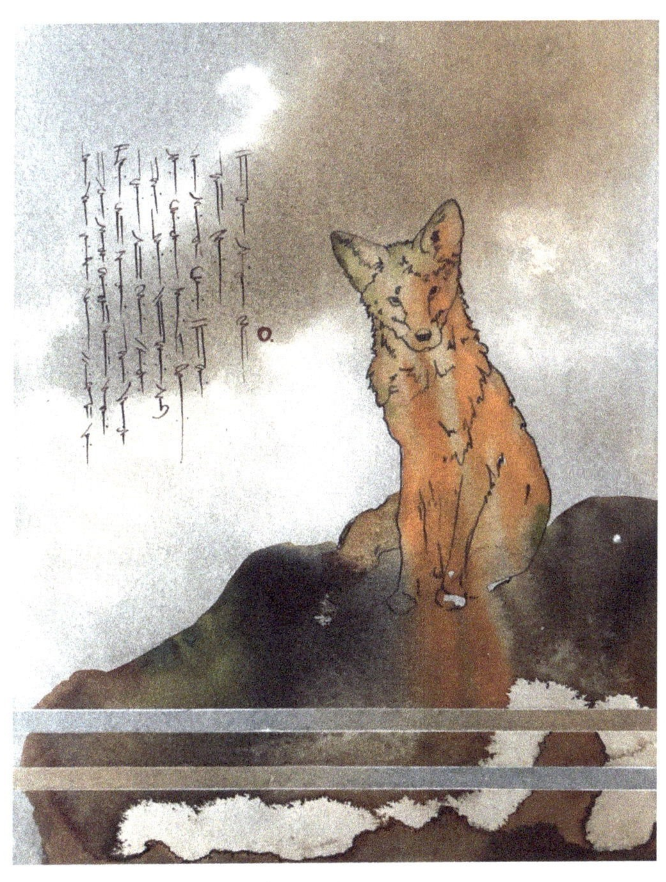

plea in the storm

Unstitched

Blue lifts first to the east:
the sky untethered.
I know the terror of seeing:
I am on my knees.
My need tastes like ground:
crossed palm reaching.
Bare wrist like an offering:
I give unto you.
My tongue like a river:
the mercy of rain.
Words unfurl like a new leaf:
my prayer rooted in this soil.
The body's ripe sorrow:
a heron lifting from the marshes.
Crows shifting on the hillside:
I plead to you.
I have been unstitched.

Dark Lands

I am [one who lives at the barren edge, larynx cut, words like plucked feathers drifting, or fox, dull tailed slipping in and out of fallen branches] silence.

Husk in a tinderbox.

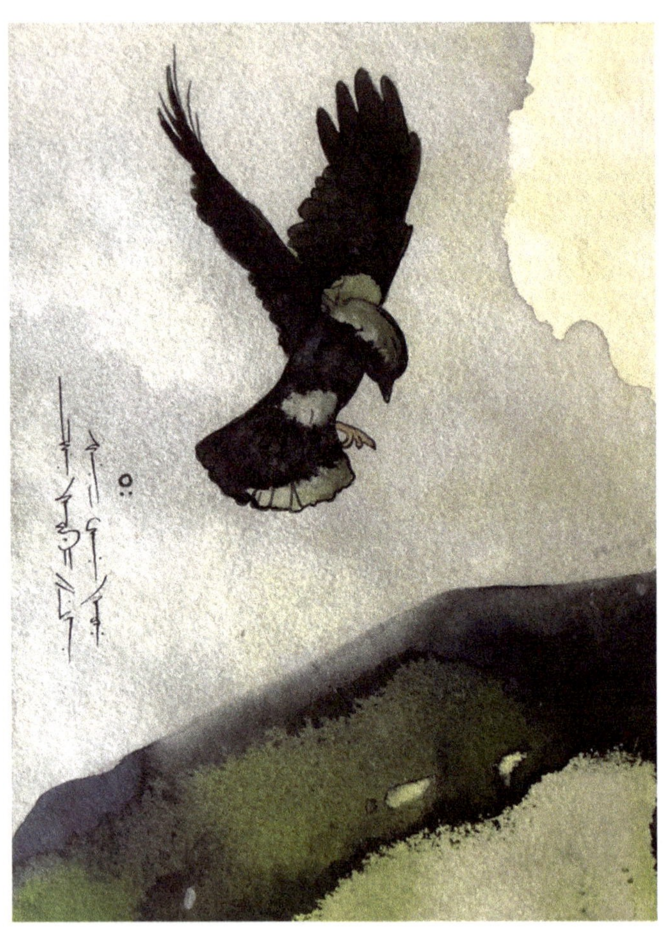

convergence, she sees

Song of the Birds

I had died the thousand small deaths
of your leaving, my heart's broken wing.

So be it. The cardinal still woke me early
with his insistent call.

And today the flocked up blackbirds
rose, turned and opened like a fan.

What seems required from the vast
blue sky is that I leap into it.

Like the cellist said, fly, fly little ones,
sing out *peace, peace, peace.*

A heart can use a little peace; take it where it comes.

I leapt.

Birds sing when they are in the sky,
they sing: "Peace, Peace, Peace."
-Pablo Casals from his speech to the UN.

Upstream

I swim the river, fish body of mine.
Slide my sleekness towand deeper pools,
water like dusk, the edge of want's seen,
what can only be found by memory.

I remember you, like a hook swallowed
line pulled taut. And now what?

Plunged into darkness all is felt by
earnest probing, gravel giving way
to root to reed to tenderness,
                    the sandy sitl.

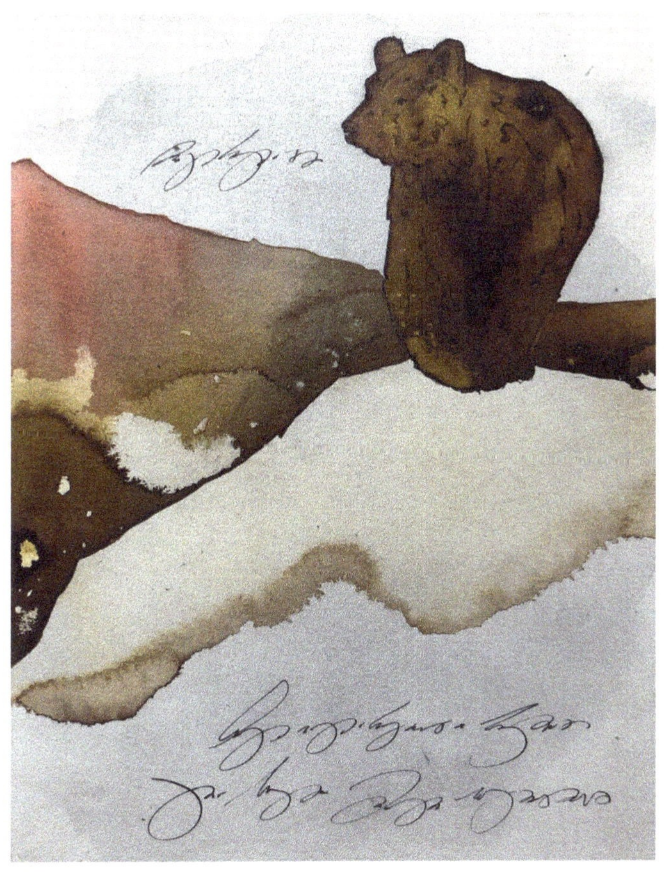

courage wakes in winter

Night Swan

So many nights
the white bird of the moon
lifts its round body across the sky,
like words in a song of love, one sung
by a Japanese courtesan, her face
painted in the waning white of loss,
round and luminous, her eyes a risen
tide, her lips red as the blood beating
through the night swan's wings.

Or is the moon a polar bear crossing
the night's sea-sky? Or the salmon's sleek
sliver running the river of darkness?

Why do I stand here at the window
thinking such lunacy? You are not here.

At the Sink

A woman who desired to make love
yearned for a thousand merciful touches
as she stood at the sink, her hands in the
warm sudsy water washing dishes. She
imagined a mighty swarm of bees descending
over her bare arms, her collarbones, the long
stretch of her neck, the wing-wind thrumming
like the breath of a lover. A thousand stinging
bodies. Her own body's reaction, apoplectic,
madness being a kind of rage, her mind vibrant
with the whir, the will, with the wanting,
drink of the gods, nectar of the bee, the long
glass neck, the bottle she clutched in her wet
hand and turned toward heaven.

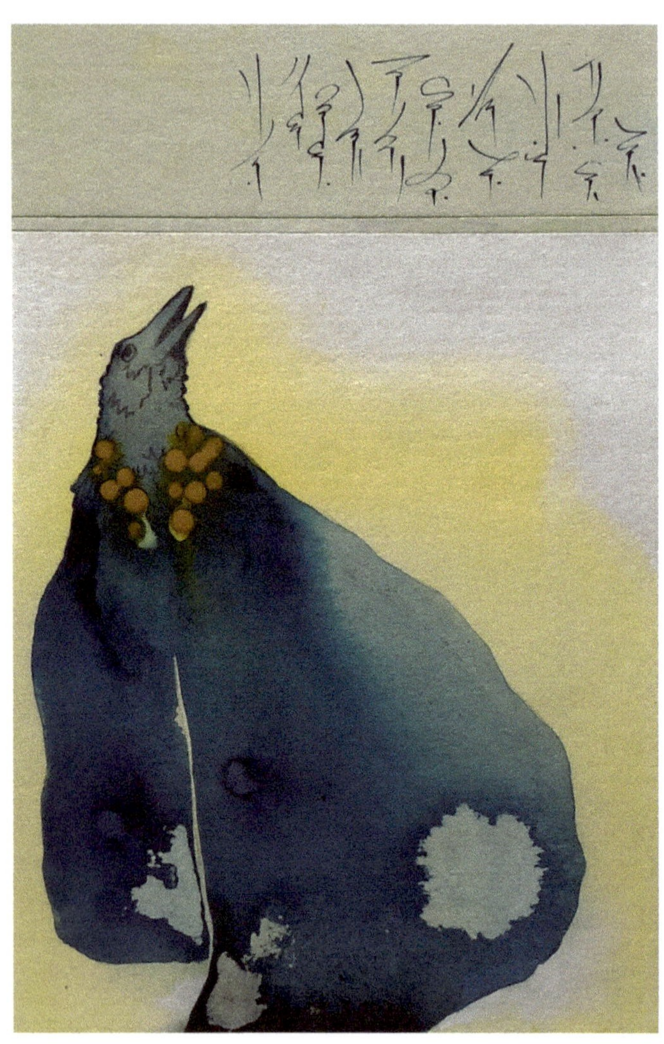

in the coming of the light

Dry Spell

So long the mountain stream's bed
has lain dry. So long my hands
have held sorrow like a grounded fish.
I have prayed for water. I have studied
the sky for sign, made my moorings there.
I have seen the sweep of black birds
turn wing for roost, the heavy clouds.

Yielding

From the branches I catch the flicking
of an eastern kingbird, it's raspy call

like lost memory on a damp wind.
In this moment all is only the bird and me,

my hand and it's wing, it's song
and the salty taste of my own words

held ablaze in my mouth. It is a mystery,
the bird and it's sharp wing that opens,

like a knife might, a yielding to your
presence in me.

Such darkness in sworn secrecy, the hidden
you give me hope to open.

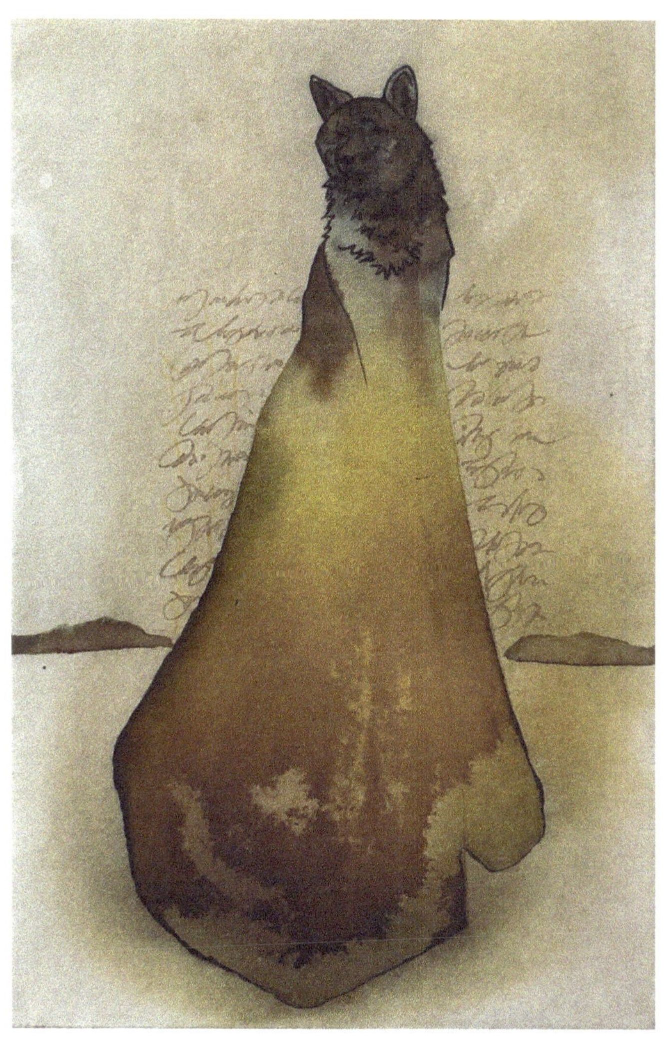

a kind of fierce light

Off Season

When your hands hesitated, circled the fields
but never landed, headed south to winter
in far off regions, silence filled my mouth, a burning cold.
My body was left land.

A season has its own torn threads. Mine are rushes
woven by wind, your hand in my hair, now empty nest.

I pray for rain; rain, for that touch on my skin. Oh,
let your fingers turn wing, let the urgency of instinct
direct you back, let you remember.

And be it that my lands warm, again, to you. That the
spring is not too late in coming.

All Night a Sky Full of Rain

By morning water has filled the low-lying lands.
In the end we will call it disaster, devastation,
wreckage and ruin, such winds, whipping.

When the flood recedes we will see what
we did not want to see, the swollen body,
the cruelty of power, of might. And innocence.

What more there is to say comes like flocking birds
from our mouths, your story and mine, gathering.
One might hope this is the dawn breaking after dark.

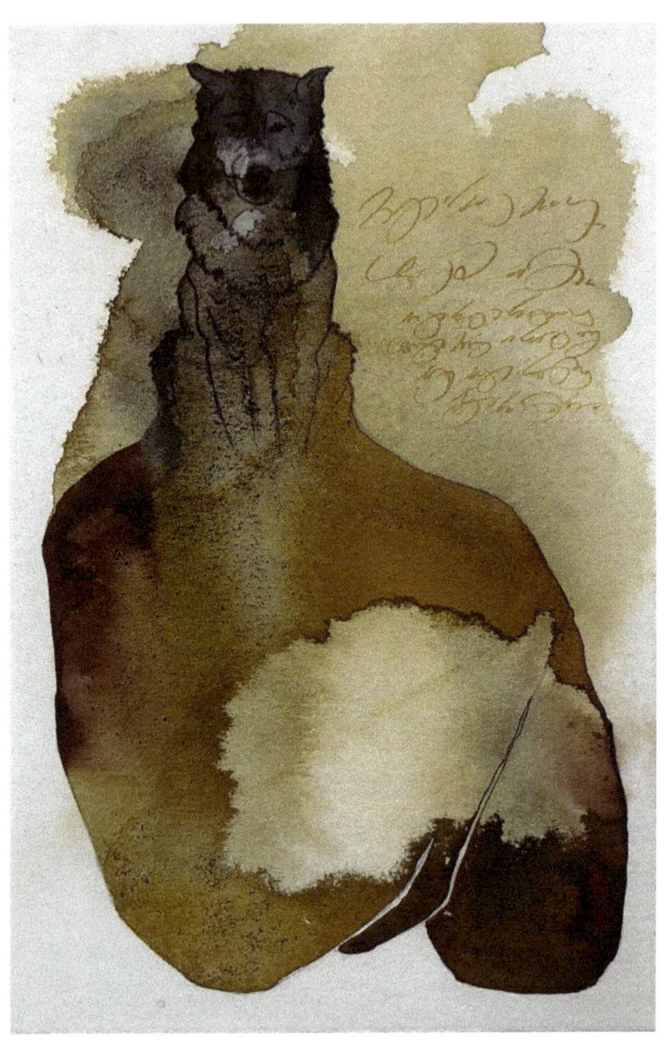

the watcher, the witness)

A Way

I went out driving to find him and found two hawks. One flying low to the field, swift and sharp. One perched high and proud. In the sloping spread of cut corn, seven does. Each one lifted her slender neck to look in my direction before turning back to graze. I found him, later, at my door come to lay down his unworthiness, like a gift, a confession. Perhaps I should have accepted, let his departure be my absolution. But my hands are like a flock of birds, all rustling spirit.

Second Thoughts

Like a flock of field sparrows,
I am back in the meadow, in grasses

and blue of chicory, the dappled white
Queen Anne's lace. That kind of a day,

always that kind of day, with you.
True, I flew like a bird, I loved, I soared.

The rain changed pitch, shifted in
the downpour. I think of walking

out my back door, walking, walking,
letting myself soak through.

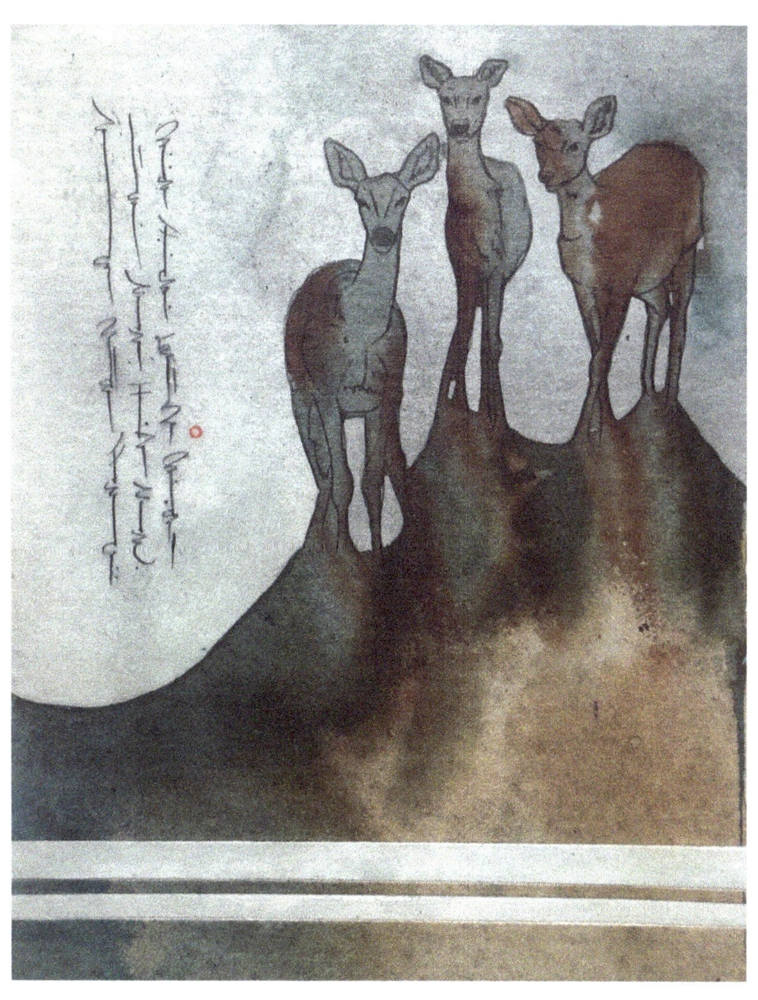

the curious

Deer's Cry

"...they saw only a herd of wild deer and let them pass by." M.P. Powers

We had prayed, sung out a cry to whom
we dared believe in: kingfisher and dove, grass
rustle and oak, the water's tumble.

It is no small thing to pack your bags and flee.
Our conviction the lorica which poured forth
in that fear's darkness.

We knew the enemy sat in wait; their intolerance honed
sharp. Put it down to our faith, or our fierce desire
to live through the night,

those who readied their swords, strung their arrows,
saw only a deer's slim body, followed by three,
four others, jump the ditch to the moon stained meadow.

We let love's flickering flame transform us, stepped
into the clearing
our delicate bones cloaked in grace.

In the Rain Grayed Evening, a Snowy Egret

... has settled, like a moon,
in the treetop. White light in our grieving.

A small grieving, in the scope of things
but any anguish leads back to that first torn sky.

Each our own storm.

Earlier we planted the yellow lily among
the green peonies, flowers like rising goldfinch.

Beneath, the stillborn kittens,
perfect little bodies which would not take breath.

We bury what we can.

It's not enough. Even the filled hole, the blossoms,
loss settling like a mist, seeps into the ground of us.

What cannot be shared or understood, private hurts
that pitch, swirl in currents of mourning.

But the moon-bird. And you.

Our hands reach for each other's over the channel,
wing their way to perch among branching fingers
like the egret's mate swooping in to land.

Devotions

I keep you like a dove under my tongue...
when I open my mouth I speak in a flock
risen and white against the sky.

There are devotions like this, on wing.
Others are like seeds; here in my hand
wild lupine.

Beloved, my heart is a parcel you open
into the wind or into the fresh earth;
into the beating blood.

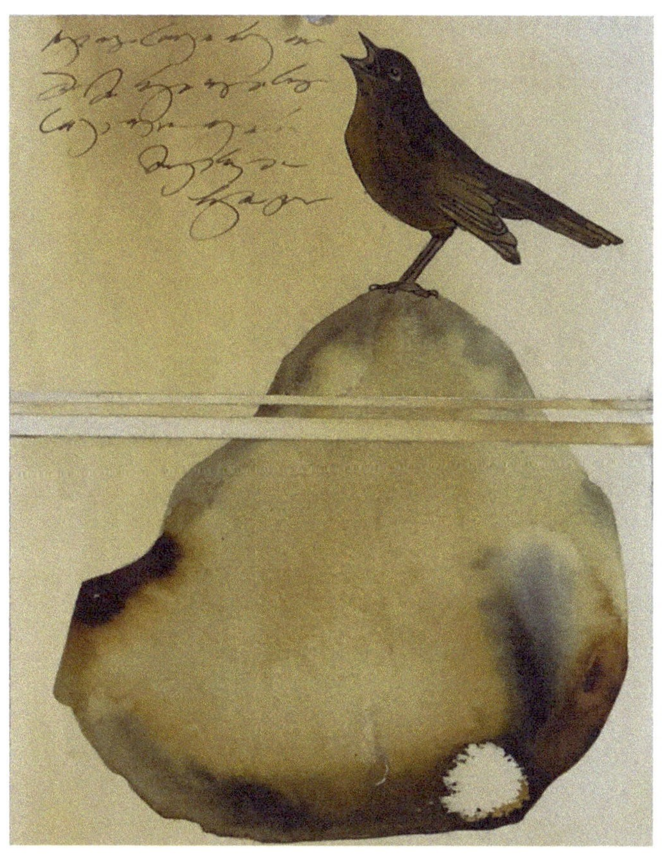

singing with the nightingale II

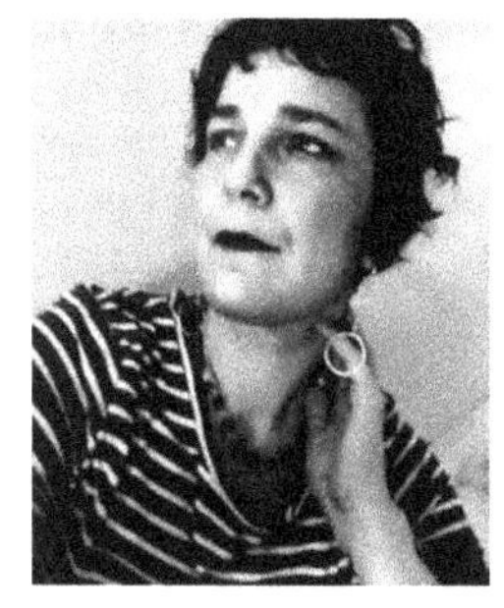

KARLA VAN VLIET is an artist, writer, gallerist, and dream-analyst. She is the author of eight collections. Her poems, asemics, and artwork have appeared worldwide. Karla is co-founder and editor of *∂eLuge Journa*l and the founder of Van Vliet Gallery, which showcases art and asemics from around the world. For more information visit vanvlietarts.com.

www.ingramcontent.com/pod-product-compliance
Lightning Source LLC
LaVergne TN
LVHW052357100826
845147LV00013B/864